UNDERSTANDING YOUR PONY

Gill Harvey
Designed by Ian McNee

Illustrated by Mikki Rain
Photographs by Kit Houghton
Consultant: Juliet Mander, BHSH

Managing editor: Felicity Brooks
Managing designer: Mary Cartwright
Front cover and page 4 photos: Bob Langrish

Contents

PONIES IN THE WILD

A domestic pony may seem very different from a wild one, but living with humans over the years hasn't changed ponies very much. They still have all the same natural instincts. So, to understand your pony properly, it does help to know how he'd live in the wild.

LIFE IN HERDS

Wild ponies live in herds which roam around, grazing. They never choose to live on their own, so any pony found on its own is probably ill or too old to keep up with the herd. Usually, a herd has one stallion, three or four mares and their foals. One of the mares makes decisions for the herd, and the stallion keeps other stallions away.

Family members

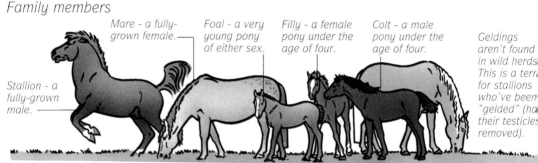

Stallion - a fully-grown male.

Mare - a fully-grown female.

Foal - a very young pony of either sex.

Filly - a female pony under the age of four.

Colt - a male pony under the age of four.

Geldings aren't found in wild herds. This is a term for stallions who've been "gelded" (had their testicles removed).

HOW PONIES SPEND THEIR TIME

Usually, ponies spend about 16 hours a day grazing. Eating small amounts all day like this is called "trickle feeding". Ponies often live in wide open places where the grass is poor, so they need to keep roaming to find enough to eat and to find water, too. Moving all the time means they get plenty of exercise and stay fit.

Ponies need to keep an eye out for danger (see "fight or flight", right), so they only sleep lying down for a total of about three hours each day. Herd members never go to sleep all at the same time. One or two always stay awake to keep guard. However, they can make up for this by dozing while they are standing up.

These Portuguese ponies are owned by local people, but lead a "wild" life most of the time.

PLAYING, ROLLING AND GROOMING

Young ponies play at fighting to learn fighting skills. This is important for colts, who will have to fight other stallions when they are older.

If he feels safe enough to expose his vulnerable belly, a pony will give his skin and coat a good scratch by lying down and rolling on the ground.

Ponies also keep their coats healthy and clean by grooming each other. They nibble each others' coats with their lips and teeth.

Ponies groom each others' backs and withers. These are areas which they can't reach themselves.

FIGHT OR FLIGHT?

Ponies are herbivores, which means they don't eat meat and are not aggressive. They are hunted by meat-eaters (predators), such as lions. Many "wild" herds are now owned by people and have few natural enemies, but they still behave cautiously. Because they run faster than most predators, their best defence has always been speed, so they deal with fear and danger by running away. If they can't flee - for example, if they are cornered - they fight as a last resort, by lashing out with kicks and bites.

HERD BEHAVIOUR

Ponies have complex ways of relating to each other. While they all have some characteristics in common, no two ponies are exactly the same. A pony's character makes a big difference to his position in the herd and to how other ponies treat him. It also makes a difference to how he relates to other animals, such as humans.

NATURAL CHARACTERISTICS

Nervousness

A pony always has to be on the look-out for danger, which makes him naturally nervous. If he has a lot of scary experiences, he tends to become even more restless and jumpy.

Curiosity

When a pony comes across something new, he doesn't feel safe until he's sure it won't harm him. If it isn't too scary, he approaches it to give it a good sniff.

Affection

Ponies know all the members of their own herd, and they like making friends (see right). They have special ways of showing affection, such as touching noses and nickering to each other.

DECIDING WHO'S BOSS OF THE HERD

Domestic groups of ponies are usually made up of mares and geldings, as most stallions are gelded. However, there is still a dominant pony or "boss" in each group, who can be a mare or a gelding. This pony makes sure that the others follow and obey her (or him).

The pecking order

All the other ponies have a position within the herd, too. They submit to ponies above them, but dominate any below. This is called the "pecking order". A pony high in the pecking order gets the best food and water, but one at the bottom, such as an ill or old pony, may be pushed away or bullied.

A pony who doesn't obey the herd "boss" is punished with nips and kicks.

FRIENDS AND RIVALS

Ponies make their own special friends within the herd. Often, friends are a pair of ponies of about the same age and height, who hold a similar position in the pecking order. Pony friends graze close together, groom each other, and protect each other if necessary.

New ponies are greeted with squeals, stamps and kicking with the front legs, and they have to be patient and submissive before they find their position in the pecking order.

In the wild, dominant ponies fight to decide who's boss. This usually happens between stallions, and the loser is driven away. If two dominant ponies are kept in a field, though, the loser can't escape. In this case it can take a while for them to sort themselves out.

Being the same height makes it easier for friends to groom each other.

HERD SQUABBLES AND "PERSONAL SPACE"

As long as a herd has sorted out its pecking order, ponies only squabble now and again. While they're grazing, each pony keeps a certain distance away from the others so as not to disturb them. This area around a pony is called "personal space", and he will drive away unwelcome ponies if they get too close (see below). It's useful to remember that ponies don't like humans fussing round them while they're eating, either.

SENSES AND THINKING

Like you, ponies have five senses: hearing, sight, touch, taste and smell. Much of the way they think is based on what they learn from their senses. They have to detect danger before it gets too close, so their sight, hearing and smell are especially good. It's also possible that they have a "sixth" sense, which alerts them to dangers humans aren't aware of.

Ponies have very good hearing partly because they can turn their ears in almost any direction.

They can turn their ears back to hear behind them, or turn just one ear to hear from two directions at once.

If your pony is listening to a noise that you can't hear, you can watch his ears to tell where it's coming from.

SMELL AND TASTE

A pony's sense of smell is good because wild ponies need to sniff out food and water as well as predators. Ponies tell each other apart by smell, and a stallion can smell a mare who is in season (ready to mate) a long way off. When he meets her, he curls his lip up (see right). This is called "Flehmen's response". A lot of ponies do this when they smell something strange, such as a lemon or garlic, as it helps them to smell it more clearly.

A pony's natural diet is not very varied, but ponies do like some foods more than others. They can also develop a liking for sweets if they are given too many.

TOUCH

A pony can't see things just in front of him because of his blind spot (see opposite page). For close-up things he relies on touch. The whiskers on his muzzle are very sensitive and tell him all he needs to know.

A pony's tail helps to swish away irritating flies.

Ponies also have sensitive skin which is easily irritated by flies, and which is ticklish in some places.

EYESIGHT

A pony has excellent eyesight, even at dusk. His eyes are on the side of his head, so he can see almost all the way around without moving his head at all. He has just two blind spots, or directions where he can't see anything. One is right in front of him, at the end of his nose, and the other is directly behind him.

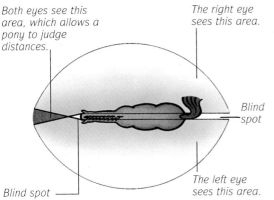

Both eyes see this area, which allows a pony to judge distances.

The right eye sees this area.

Blind spot

The left eye sees this area.

Blind spot

THE "SIXTH SENSE"

Ponies do seem to have a strange way of knowing when something exciting or bad is happening. They also seem to know how humans are feeling, and they are especially good at picking up tension and fear.

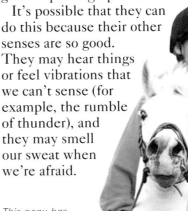

It's possible that they can do this because their other senses are so good. They may hear things or feel vibrations that we can't sense (for example, the rumble of thunder), and they may smell our sweat when we're afraid.

This pony has noticed something his rider isn't aware of.

HOW DOES YOUR PONY THINK?

A pony's thinking is based partly on his instincts, and partly on his experiences (what his senses tell him). His experience teaches him that some things are "good", and other things are "bad".

It's important to realize, though, that he doesn't work this out logically. A bad thing is anything that scares or hurts him the first time he comes across it. For example, a plastic bag blowing around may make him afraid of all plastic bags from then on.

However, his strong herd instincts mean he may trust the experience of other ponies and humans, if they are kind. In this way, he may learn to overcome his fear.

A young pony can learn from an older one that something such as learning to jump is not as difficult or scary as it looks.

PONY LANGUAGE

You can tell a lot about how your pony is feeling by watching his expression and the shape of his body (his "body language"), and by listening to the sounds he makes. The more you watch, the more you will see that he looks quite different depending on his mood.

BODY LANGUAGE

A pony's mood usually shows in his face, especially his ears and eyes. However, he also shows how he is feeling with his whole body. Important clues are given by how he holds his head, neck and tail, and by how tense his muscles are.

Anger and submission

This picture could be of two ponies galloping playfully, but if you look closer, you can see that one is feeling angry and aggressive, while the other is afraid and submissive.

This pony is the angry one. His ears are back, and his nostrils are flared. His neck is thrusted towards the other pony and his tail swishes out behind him.

This pony is submissive. Although he's galloping, his tail is held much lower. His head is tucked in towards his chest, giving his neck a stiff, tense look. His ears are laid back, but out of fear, not anger.

Excitement

An excited pony makes a very upright, jaunty shape. Ponies also look like this when they are showing off and flirting with each other.

His ears are pricked forwards and his eyes are alert, bright and interested.

His tail is held high, but it's not swishing angrily.

His head is held high, his neck is arched and his posture is very alert. He's ready to spring into action.

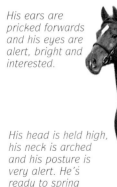

Relaxation

A relaxed pony makes a long, low shape, though he can jump out of it quickly if something catches his attention. If he doesn't, he may be ill (see pages 14-15).

His ears flick in different directions, and his eyes are half-open, showing that he is almost dozing.

His tail is held quite low, but it's not clamped hard against his body.

His head and neck droop slightly, and his mouth looks relaxed.

All his muscles look relaxed.

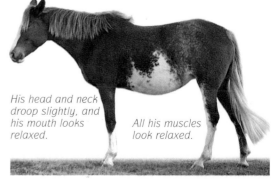

SIGNS TO WATCH OUT FOR

Ears laid back - this is sure to be a bad sign. It is one of the first signs that he is annoyed or unhappy about something.

Showing the whites of his eyes, flared nostrils - he is feeling afraid or nervous. He is also likely to hold his head high and his neck tense.

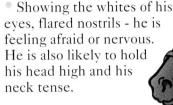

Lifting a back leg, or turning his hind quarters - watch out! He is about to kick, especially if his ears are back as well.

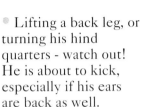

Pawing and stamping the ground - he may be frustrated, or want feeding. Sometimes it is a sign of colic (see page 15).

Tossing head, swishing tail - it may be the flies, but he could be frustrated or annoyed. If he's annoyed, his overall body language will be tense.

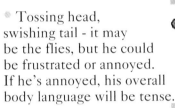

Thrusting his head, snapping and nipping are signs of aggression, though sometimes ponies nip playfully.

Flicking ears - he is listening to different noises. If they are droopy, he may be relaxed. If they are cold as well, he may be feeling off-colour.

Clamped down tail, held low - he is either cold, ill or afraid of something behind him. It is also a sign of submission.

PONY NOISES

Neighing

A neigh is a general call between ponies when they are some distance apart. They also neigh when they are upset, for example when they have to leave a friend.

Snorting

Snorting is usually a sign of nervousness or fear, for example when a pony comes across an unusual object, or sometimes an unusual smell.

Nickering

Nickering, or snickering, is a low noise of welcome. A mare nickers to her foal, and pony friends nicker to each other. Your pony may nicker to greet you, too.

Squealing

Ponies squeal when they are excited, for example when they meet another pony for the first time. Stallions also squeal to mares in season.

Some ponies neigh more than others.

YOU AND YOUR PONY

To live happily with humans, a pony needs to feel safe and secure. In the wild, being with other ponies makes him feel safe, but if he's domesticated, humans become part of his "herd", too. So, to relate to him well, you need to build on the trust and loyalty that herd members have for each other.

GETTING TO KNOW EACH OTHER

A pony is happiest when he understands his pecking order and knows who's boss. Having a leader makes him feel secure, so he is quite willing to be told what to do. This is why it's your job to be "herd leader". If you're not, he may think he has to make his own decisions, which will lead to a lot of confusion and fighting between you.

Being leader doesn't mean frightening or bullying him. It means being firm, but kind and affectionate, so that he sees you as a friend as well.

To act as leader, keep your commands clear and simple so that he knows exactly what you want. When he behaves well, pat him and praise him in a pleased tone of voice. If he's naughty, tell him off in an angry voice. You can slap him on the neck if he bites or kicks, but never hit his head or he will become afraid of having it touched, or "headshy".

You will soon get to know his character and moods. He will come to recognize you and your voice, and he'll learn to understand when you're pleased with him.

ARE YOU UP TO THE JOB?

A pony knows when he can get the better of someone. If you are not up to being herd leader, you will have constant trouble. For this reason, it is important to have a pony that matches your abilities, and not one that's too much of a handful. You need to be sure that you can give him plenty of attention, too. Once he has accepted that you are his herd leader, a pony will rely on you for protection, care and affection. If you can't meet these needs (for example, if you don't have enough time) you should think about letting someone else look after him.

This pony doesn't want to turn and follow his owner, so he pulls away as she pulls him back.

She tells him off for pulling and doesn't give way, keeping up the pressure to make him turn.

He is still resisting, with his ears laid back. She still won't let him get away with it.

The pony realizes she's boss and gives up. He follows and she praises him for being good.

GOOD HANDLING

Ponies are good at telling what time it is and will look forward to your visits.

Remember that your pony can't see what's directly behind him. Always approach his shoulder, so he can see you easily.

Talk to him quietly and move calmly so that you don't startle him. Jerky, sudden movements will frighten him.

Watch him carefully on a daily basis to learn his body language. This will also help you tell if he's acting unusually.

Show him affection, as other ponies would - scratch his back and withers, and talk to him in a soft voice.

A domestic pony doesn't have much freedom, which is stressful for him. It helps if he knows what to expect, though, which is why it's important to keep to a routine. Try to muck out and feed him at the same time each day.

KEYS TO DEVELOPING TRUST

* Be consistent. Don't tell him off for something one day, then ignore it the next. Stick to a daily routine. He'll get upset if you keep changing it.

* Don't spoil him. If you give him titbits every time he asks and let him get away with things, he will lose respect for you and start misbehaving.

* Spend time with him. If you only see him when you ride, you won't get to know each other. Remember his personal space, though, and don't swamp him too much.

DAILY LIFE

Ponies that live with humans can't look after themselves in the way they would in the wild. We change their natural lifestyle by riding them, confining them in small spaces, and even deciding what they eat. To keep a pony happy and healthy, it's important to make up for these differences as much as possible.

STABLED PONIES

Living in a stable is the most unnatural way for a pony to live. A stabled pony isn't free to exercise, he can't graze and can't search for more food if he runs out. He can't mix with other ponies, and living in a small enclosed space is not very good for his health, especially if it's dusty. Bear all these things in mind when you plan his stable, so that you can meet as many of his needs as possible.

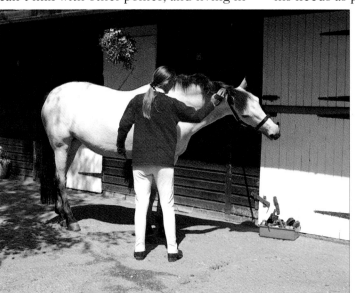

Exercise
Ponies exercise naturally if they are grazing, but they can get bored and unfit living in a stable. This can lead to problems (see pages 14-15). To prevent this, turn your pony out as much as possible, and ride him every day if you can.

Grooming
A stabled pony can't roll to groom himself. He doesn't have pony friends to groom him either, so you need to give him a good groom every day to keep his skin and muscles healthy.

Space
The stable should be big enough for him to move around in and at least 4 x 4m (12 x 12ft).

Bedding
Stables often have hard floors that a pony may hurt himself on when he lies down, so make sure his bedding is deep. Bear in mind that dry, dusty bedding can cause health problems (see page 15).

Ventilation
Ponies naturally live out in the fresh air, so they need plenty of ventilation. Always leave the top door and any air vents open. If it's cold give him a rug - don't shut the top door.

Food and water
He should always have plenty of fresh water and hay. Remember that in the wild, grazing would keep him busy nearly all day.

PONIES AT GRASS

Living in a field is more natural than living in a stable, but still not as natural as you might think. A field is much smaller than the open spaces a wild pony can roam, and it usually doesn't have natural sources of water, shade or shelter. It also tends to get soft and muddy in winter, and to grow too much lush grass in spring.

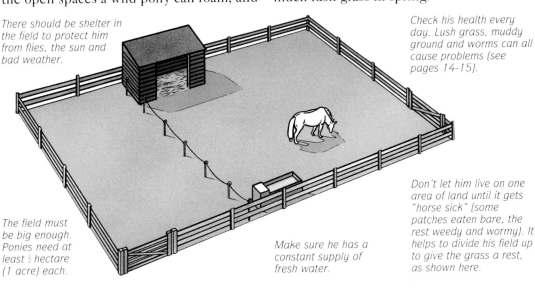

There should be shelter in the field to protect him from flies, the sun and bad weather.

Check his health every day. Lush grass, muddy ground and worms can all cause problems (see pages 14-15).

The field must be big enough. Ponies need at least ½ hectare (1 acre) each.

Make sure he has a constant supply of fresh water.

Don't let him live on one area of land until it gets "horse sick" (some patches eaten bare, the rest weedy and wormy). It helps to divide his field up to give the grass a rest, as shown here.

IS YOUR PONY LONELY?

Your pony won't be very happy if he's kept on his own, even if you visit him regularly. Ideally, he should be kept with other ponies for company. If he's stabled, he should at least be able to see other ponies.

If you must keep him on his own, try to make up for it in other ways. If he lives out, try giving him other company such as a sheep or cow. If he lives in, keep visiting him and get other people to visit him too.

Introductions

When you introduce your pony to strange ponies, you can avoid problems by doing it gradually.

If he is going to share a field with several ponies, it helps to introduce him to just one or two of the friendlier ones first.

If possible, let him meet a new pony over a safe fence or gate, so that they can't kick out at each other.

These two ponies are being introduced over a gate.

GOOD HEALTH

Part of knowing your pony well is being able to spot when he's out of sorts. You may even be able to prevent many common problems before they arise. If in doubt, though, always consult a vet rather than try to guess what's wrong.

DAILY HEALTH CHECK

You should check your pony over every day for signs of pain or ill health. He can't tell you if something's wrong, so you must watch for anything unusual in his appearance or behaviour. If you are used to his body language and how he normally looks and behaves, you should be able to tell if he is ill just by looking at him.

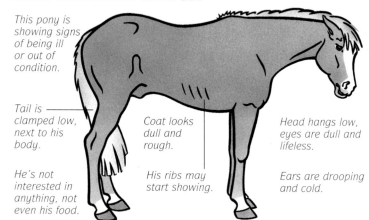

This pony is showing signs of being ill or out of condition.

Tail is clamped low, next to his body.

Coat looks dull and rough.

Head hangs low, eyes are dull and lifeless.

He's not interested in anything, not even his food.

His ribs may start showing.

Ears are drooping and cold.

Health checklist

• Watch him walk to check he's not lame. If a front leg is lame, he will nod his head slightly as he walks.

• Run a hand down each leg to check for any swellings, lumps or cuts, or areas that feel hotter than usual.

• Check that his eyes are bright, with no runny discharge. Gently lift an eyelid to check that the membrane is pink.

• Check his feet for cuts. Make sure his shoes fit him properly, and that his frog is clean and healthy-looking.

• Check that his nose does not have a runny discharge. If it does, he may have a cold or other infection.

• Watch how he eats. If he dribbles or lets food drop out of his mouth, he may have a problem with his teeth.

• Check his coat for any odd-looking patches or spots, and check for sores on the saddle and girth areas.

• Look at his teeth, especially if he's not eating properly. Look for obvious problems such as jagged edges.

COMMON HEALTH PROBLEMS

When a pony is stabled, he may develop problems with his breathing and digestion, and his legs may also become stiff from standing in one place. For grass-kept ponies, laminitis (see below) is a common problem. Your pony will stand a much better chance of complete recovery if you can spot these things before they get too serious.

	Symptoms	Causes	Prevention	Treatment
Colic	Restless, sweating, tries to roll. Paws ground. Doesn't eat. Looks round at belly and kicks it.	Exercise soon after feed, or feed soon after exercise. Poor quality feed. Unbalanced routine. Worms. Very rich grass or concentrates.	Keep to routine. Feed plenty of hay, not too many concentrates. Don't feed too soon before or after exercise. Give him plenty of exercise. Worm regularly.	Call the vet. Allow him to lie down in stable with lots of deep bedding. If he tries to roll, keep him standing and walk him around gently.
Coughs	Coughing. Runny nose. No energy, puffs when exercised. May have a temperature if it's an infection.	If the cough is due to infection, he may have caught it from strange ponies. It's more likely to be an allergy, or because he's out of condition from dusty or poor quality feed, dusty bedding, poor ventilation or confinement.	If infection or chill, keep him warm with a rug and isolate. Vaccinate against infections. If due to bedding, change to less dusty bedding, such as wood chips or paper. Check ventilation, and quality of feed. Soak his hay.	Call the vet. Allow pony plenty of rest to recover before working him hard. Make as many changes as you can to his stable, bedding and feed (see prevention), and turn out as much as possible.
Laminitis	Pony is lame. One or both front feet are hot. Pony tries to take weight off toes by stretching legs out and standing on heels.	Too much rich spring grass or other rich food.	Don't allow to eat too much spring grass - bring into stable if necessary. Give plenty of exercise.	Call the vet. Bring pony into stable. Give plenty of soft bedding that he can't eat, such as wood chips. Cool feet down in cold water. If very bad, allow to rest, otherwise exercise gently on soft surface.
Mud fever	Skin around heels is sore, cracked and scabby. Infection may have led to cracks spreading up legs. Heels are hot and swollen. May be lame.	Field too wet and muddy, chapping skin which becomes infected.	Wash legs gently with slightly medicated water and dry carefully. Get correct ointment from vet. Call the vet if it worsens, or if your pony becomes lame.	Don't allow pony to stay out in a very muddy field - change field or bring him in when it's very muddy. Protect legs and heels with barrier cream.

LIFESTYLE PROBLEMS

Some ponies find domestic life more stressful than others, so if your pony starts to develop a bad habit, he may be responding to stress. It doesn't make him a "bad" pony. He may have had a bad experience, feel lonely, bored or trapped. Watch out for any warning signs, because once he has a habit, it can be difficult to cure him of it.

"BAD TEMPERED" PONIES

Biting, kicking, barging and being generally unco-operative in the paddock or stable can become nasty habits if you let them continue. If your pony acts this way with you or other ponies, there may be a number of reasons why.

With you
● Remember his "flight or fight" instinct. He may be afraid of you, or feeling trapped. You need to reassure him and work on getting him to trust you.
● He may know he can get the better of you. You must be very firm and say "No!" If necessary, give him a slap on his neck.
● He may be spoilt and expects treats all the time. You need to say "No!" and stop spoiling him.
● He may be demanding attention through being bored or hungry.
● If he's usually good-natured, he may be in pain. Get him checked by a vet.

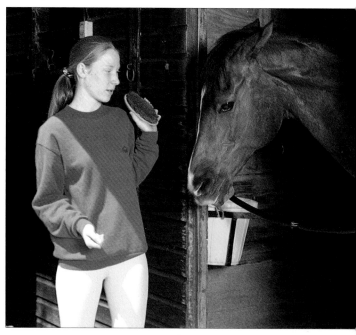

If your pony tries to bite you, it's natural to jump back, as shown here. However, you must tell him off to let him know he can't get away with it.

With other ponies
● If he's only aggressive with one other pony, it may be a personality clash. Keep the two ponies apart.

● He may be working out his place in the pecking order. If the ponies have only just met, don't worry, as they will probably sort themselves out. Check him after a few days to make sure that he has found a position in the group.

● There may not be enough food, space or water to go round, leading to squabbles. In this case, ponies lower in the pecking order won't get a fair share of food or water, so it's very important to sort the problem out.
● He may just be very touchy about his personal space, and snap at ponies who get too close.

STABLE STRESS AND BOREDOM

If your pony develops a stable "vice", practical, short-term measures can help (see table below). However, you should still treat the cause of the problem by improving his living conditions as much as possible.

* Ride, or exercise him, every day.
* Give him plenty of hay to keep him busy, and don't give him too much rich food unless he gets enough exercise to burn it off.
* Turn him out for as much of the day as possible.

* Keep to a routine.
* Make sure he can see out of the stable.
* Give him some toys to play with, such as a ball that he can kick around.
* Make sure he gets plenty of company (other ponies or humans).

	Problem	Practical/short-term solution
Weaving	Pony swings his head to and fro constantly. May also rock to and fro on his front legs. If he rocks, the stress on his legs may make him lame.	An anti-weave grille fitted to his stable door may stop him swinging his head. He may just move further back and carry on weaving, in which case you can only try to get to the root of the problem (see above).
Crib-biting, windsucking	When he crib-bites, a pony holds on to the top of the stable door and chews at it. He may also suck air into his stomach, called windsucking. Crib-biting eventually damages teeth, and windsucking makes it harder for him to digest his food, causing indigestion or colic.	To stop him crib-biting, you can attach a strip of metal to the top of the stable door so that he cannot chew it, or paint the door with nasty-tasting anti-chew fluid. There are special collars that go around his neck to stop him windsucking.
Box-walking	The pony walks around and around the stable without stopping.	Check that he is not in pain. If the problem is boredom or stress, try placing objects (for example, tyres or bales of straw) in the stable that he has to step around.
Door-banging	He regularly kicks at his door or stable walls, which can damage his legs as well as the door. The noise may upset other ponies too.	Protect his legs by padding the door with something soft, like rubber matting. This doesn't make as much noise, which is partly what he likes, so he may stop.

A PONY'S TRAINING

You may not have known your pony when he was young, but if he is well-behaved this is almost certainly because he had good experiences as a foal. If you have problems with him, it may be worth finding out who trained him, and how.

THE LEARNING PROCESS

The best way to train a pony is to build on his natural process of learning through experience (see page 7). After a new experience, he remembers whether it is good or bad for a long time. His training should therefore be full of positive experiences that he is happy to repeat.

New things should be introduced gently, with plenty of time for him to get over his fear.

If he gets scared while learning something, he should be taken back to an earlier stage until he's happy again. He should be allowed to grasp each lesson and repeat it lots of times before he's moved on to the next.

If he's good, he should be praised and patted (titbits will spoil him). If he misbehaves, he must be told off firmly, but he should never be frightened badly.

EARLY EXPERIENCES

Ideally, learning to accept domestic life starts as soon as a pony is born. If he's used to being handled well when he's very young, he learns to trust humans naturally. This makes it much easier for him to accept the later stages of his training.

A foal's first step is to learn that humans won't hurt him, so he should be handled gently, firmly and as soon as possible after birth.

Next, he's taught to walk calmly alongside his trainer when he's being led. When he responds well, his trainer praises him with lots of pats.

Soon, he learns about grooming, and that humans can touch vulnerable places such as his belly and head without hurting him.

18

THE FARRIER

If he is used to having his legs and feet touched and groomed, a pony should have no problem learning to stand for a farrier. This does involve strange objects and actions that may frighten him, though, so his trainer should be at hand all the time to calm and reassure him.

ACCEPTING A BRIDLE

A pony is introduced to a bit and bridle when he's about two. If he's used to wearing a halter, this won't come as a big surprise. It still needs introducing carefully, though, as he mustn't get the idea that it can hurt him. At first, the bridle shouldn't have a noseband or reins, and should be put on very gently.

If it's introduced properly, the bit will seem like a toy that he can play with in his mouth.

LEARNING TO LOAD

A trailer or box is a dark, spooky place for a pony, and the ramp feels very unstable.

Let your pony inspect the ramp. If you're loading him for the first time, a bridle will give you more control.

If he learns early on that it's safe, it will save a lot of stress later. He should be given plenty of time to inspect the ramp before he steps onto it, and if possible the front of the trailer should be opened up, so that he can see through it. The idea is to coax him gently onto the ramp, so everyone should stay calm and patient. If necessary, he can be encouraged with some tasty food.

GOING TO SHOWS

A pony can be taken to shows long before he's ready to be ridden, as being used to all the strange sights and sounds is good experience for when he's older.

He can be entered in an in-hand showing class, (a class for ponies that are led, not ridden) or he can just go along for the experience. If possible, an older pony should be taken to stay near him for the day. This will give him more confidence and help keep him calm.

Going to shows is tiring for a young pony, so he shouldn't be taken too often.

19

ACCEPTING A RIDER

To an untrained pony, a rider is a scary, heavy object which he can't see properly, and in the wild, the only similar thing he'd come across would be a predator on his back. So, this stage in his training takes very careful preparation.

GETTING USED TO A SADDLE

Introduction to a saddle or lunging "roller" takes place when the pony is about three. First, he should be given a good look at it.

Next it can be put on his back, very gently. The girth should be done up just enough to stop it slipping, never tightly or suddenly.

He may try bucking the saddle off, but this is fine. Once he is convinced that it can't harm him, he begins to get used to it.

LUNGING

Lunging is a very important part of a pony's training. It helps to develop the muscles, flexibility and balanced posture that he'll need for carrying a rider.

The pony moves in a circle around his trainer, who controls him with a lunge line and whip. He is taught to obey the trainer's voice, and the sound of the whip teaches him to move forward on command. In order to make sure that the muscles on both sides of his body are developing properly, he spends time circling in both directions.

After a while, side reins are added. They are attached to his bit and to rings on the saddle. This creates contact with his mouth, preparing him for a rider holding the reins.

LONG REINING

When a pony has been lunged for a while, he is introduced to long reining. Two long lines go from the bit, through the stirrups and back to the trainer, who walks behind. The trainer is positioned slightly to one side of the pony's blind spot. This means he can just see her, but has to go forward independently in response to the aids, as he will have to do when he has a rider.

Long reining teaches him to move forward in a straight line.

THE BACKING PROCESS

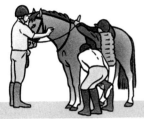

One person holds the pony while someone else is given a leg up, putting pressure on his back.

Next, the rider lies right across the pony's back so that the pony can feel her full weight.

The rider now sits astride, but lies flat at first in case the pony is frightened by seeing her there.

Once the pony is used to feeling the rider, she can sit up straight, keeping still in the saddle.

Next, the pony is led around on the lunge rein. The rider holds the reins, but doesn't take up any contact.

Eventually, the rider begins to put pressure on the pony's sides, and makes gentle contact with his mouth.

Essentials for backing

* As with all training, the trainers should be very knowledgeable and experienced.
* All trainers must wear protective clothing - hats, gloves, and a back protector for the rider.
* Lessons should be kept short, so that the pony doesn't get bored or upset.
* The pony's reactions should be watched carefully. If he reacts badly, he should be taken back to an earlier stage to gain more confidence.
* Every lesson should finish on a positive note.

THE OUTSIDE WORLD

For a pony to be safe for less experienced riders, he must be used to coping with the outside world. He must be confident enough to trust his rider when something startles or frightens him.

He can be prepared for frightening or unusual objects by being introduced to them at home where he feels safe. When he is first ridden out, it can help if he has a steady, older pony for company.

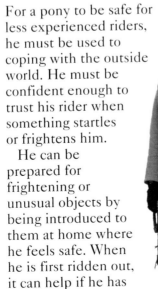

By being allowed to investigate this black plastic bag, the pony realizes it won't hurt him.

GOOD RIDING

If a pony has been backed properly, you shouldn't have too many problems riding him. It's up to you to ride confidently and well. If you build a good working relationship with him, he shouldn't develop bad habits and will remain a pleasure to ride.

USING YOUR AIDS

Your pony should have learned to respond to the five natural aids, which are your legs, voice, hands, seat and body. You shouldn't need artificial aids, such as a whip, unless your pony is very lazy or stubborn, and spurs are only needed for advanced riding.

This pony is responding well to his rider's aids.

- Keep your leg commands clear and simple, and keep your weight steady in the saddle. If you keep kicking, moving your legs around and shifting your weight, he won't know what you're trying to tell him.
- Keep steady contact with his mouth, enough for him to feel it but not enough to hurt him. Don't fuss around with the reins.
- Use your voice clearly. Change your tone when you are pleased or angry with him, and give him instructions firmly.

A BALANCED SEAT

Having a rider on his back upsets a pony's natural balance, but he can regain it if his hocks are under him (called engaging his hocks) and his neck is flexed properly.
A well-balanced seat helps him to do these things, and makes your weight less uncomfortable for him.

Riding without stirrups helps to develop a firm and well-balanced seat.

WATCH YOUR RIDING

If you ride lazily, your pony will probably become lazy too. If you think about your riding and try to improve, you will be less likely to blame your pony for things which are really your fault. Check your legs, hands and seat as you ride, and work out what messages you are giving.

Doing exercises in the saddle is one way of improving your riding.

RESPECTING HIS LIMITS

When you ask your pony to do something new, remember that he learns by experience. This means that he won't understand why you want him to do it.

Instead, he will learn by being encouraged and praised for getting it right, and being corrected when he gets it wrong. This process can take a while, so you must be very patient.

Working your pony over trotting poles may not seem exciting, but it helps him to develop his skills.

Don't overstretch him

If you push your pony too far or too fast, he may lose confidence and so begin to lose trust in you. It's important to understand and respect his limits, and not to ask more of him than you know is possible. He can't read your mind, so being asked to do things he doesn't understand will only confuse him.

REMEMBER WHO'S BOSS

Even if he has been well trained, a pony will naturally try to get his own way if he can. It's up to you to make sure he stays in the right position in the pecking order, with you at the top. Don't let him get away with lazy habits or with playing up. If he knows you are boss, he will respect and trust you more in the long run.

Running out at jumps is a favourite trick of naughty ponies, and a sure sign that your pony doesn't have much respect for your riding.

CONSISTENCY

One of the most important qualities that a rider can have is consistency. This means treating him in the same way every day and in every situation, so that he knows what to expect. If you let him get away with something one day, he will be very upset if you punish him for it the next.

Keeping him confident

* Ride confidently, so that he knows you are sure about what you want him to do.
* Stop working before he gets tired and stale, and finish work on a positive note.
* Reassure him if he gets confused and tense. Take him back to an earlier stage.
* Always think before you tell him off. Was it really his fault - or yours?

BAD COMMUNICATION

Most ponies play up from time to time, especially if they are lively and spirited. However, this is often because of bad riding and communication, not because they're being naughty. If your pony is not going well, you need to look carefully at your own skills before blaming him. You should also check that he's not in pain (see pages 26-27).

RIDING PROBLEMS

This pony is resisting his rider and fighting for his head. His swishing tail shows he's upset. His rider needs to work out why.

Remember that carrying a rider isn't natural for your pony. When he's ridden badly, he can quickly lose his co-ordination. He'll start poking his nose out and trailing his legs behind him.

An undeveloped seat

If your seat is unbalanced, you put a strain on your pony's back, making him tense up. You are more likely to bounce around heavily in the saddle, which can make his back sore. You may also hurt his mouth by balancing yourself with the reins and jabbing him with the bit. It's not really surprising if he becomes unsettled and unco-operative as a result.

Mixed messages

If your riding skills aren't all they could be, it's very easy to confuse your pony with conflicting aids. You may be telling him one thing with your hands and another with your seat and legs. He will fight because he doesn't know what to do.

This sort of problem can get worse if he is then told off for not doing the right thing. To him, you're just being unfair, and he'll begin to lose his trust in you.

This rider is urging the pony on with her legs, but holding him back with the reins. As a result, his ears are back, his nose is in the air and his back is "hollow".

This pony has just refused. He may be playing up, but refusals are often the rider's fault. Telling him off makes him even more unhappy and confused.

LACK OF CONFIDENCE

Yours

Your pony's "sixth sense" means that he can tell if you lack confidence. He relies on your guidance, so if you're nervous, it will worry him and make him nervous too. You're also less likely to ride well if you're all tensed up.

Your pony's

Inexperienced or young ponies tend to lack confidence. However, poor riding, bad experiences, and having too much demanded of them can make older ponies lose confidence too.

Ponies often refuse because they can tell that their rider isn't confident about jumping a fence.

FINDING A SOLUTION

If your riding needs improvement, ask an instructor to watch you ride. She should be able to spot any problems with your seat or aids. You could go back to being lunged for a while to iron out your problems.

If you need to build up your pony's confidence, take him back to a basic stage where he is sure of what he is doing, and build up his work very gradually from there.

Is he the right pony?

It may be that your pony is too big or too high-spirited for you. If you continue riding him without being able to control him or keep him balanced, he is likely to lose confidence and even develop bad habits. It's a better idea to ride a quiet, experienced pony until your own skills have developed.

Riding on a lunge again allows you to concentrate on your seat.

Many problems arise from riding a pony that's the wrong size for you. Riding one that's too small isn't a good idea as it puts him under strain and leads to lazy riding habits.

PROBLEM HABITS

Sometimes a minor riding or handling difficulty can develop into a real problem, or even a serious bad habit. Some problems can be managed and cured with understanding, careful handling and retraining, but other habits need expert help.

IS HE IN PAIN?

Pain is one of the most common reasons for a pony's bad behaviour, especially if he's usually good. He can't tell you where he's in pain, or why - he just tries to avoid the problem. Check him for signs of discomfort. If an area is sore, he'll flinch when you run your hand over it. If you can't spot anything, have him checked by an expert.

Common sore spots

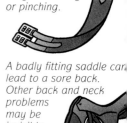

Teeth can get jagged if they're not regularly rasped, and catch on the inside of the pony's mouth.

A pony can suffer a lot of discomfort from his girth chafing or pinching.

Problems in the legs and feet are fairly easily spotted, as the pony usually goes lame. Call your vet to check what's wrong.

A badly fitting saddle can lead to a sore back. Other back and neck problems may be invisible, so consult an expert.

Problems with your pony's teeth can be avoided by asking your vet to check his mouth regularly.

WHAT'S HE AFRAID OF?

If you are sure your pony isn't in pain, you need to find out whether he's unhappy or afraid of something.

If he seems afraid of one thing in particular, he may have had a bad experience of it in the past, or more recently if his fear develops suddenly. He may have been trained poorly, or his training may be unfinished. He may even have been treated badly.

He may be unhappy if his home unsettles him, for example if he's being bullied or if his stableyard is very noisy. He may also become irritable and jumpy if he's fed too much rich food.

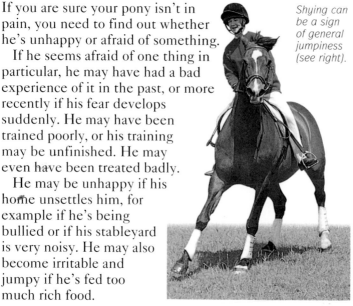

Shying can be a sign of general jumpiness (see right).

TREATING PROBLEMS

Remember that one bad experience, which you may quickly forget, can have a big effect on your pony. In addition, problems caused by pain can continue when he's better, as he's learnt a new way of behaving.

● Don't underestimate how much an experience may affect your pony. Give him time to get over pain or fear, and retrain him carefully.

● Don't start telling him off for bad behaviour until you are sure he is not in pain or afraid - you will only add to his unhappiness.

PULLING AND JOGGING

If a pony is excited it's natural for him to pull a little. However, if he's always jogging along with his head in the air, there's something wrong. Pain from his teeth, back or tack are common causes, but once you're sure he's fine, you need to look at your riding. If you're tense, you may be pulling, which is making him pull too. He may also have become insensitive to your aids if they're not clear.

What to do
- Do some basic schooling with an instructor.
- Keep your hands still.
- Don't stop using your legs. Ride him strongly, but try not to get tensed up.
- Feed him fewer concentrates. Ride him often to burn off his energy.

A jogger may need retraining, so he knows when to walk or trot.

SHYING

A pony's instincts tell him to shy when he spots something spooky. The odd shy is fine, but if it's a habit you need to work on calming him down.

What to do
- Try to spot a scary object before he does, then turn his head away from it and ride him forward strongly.
- If he's seen it, let him inspect the scary object.
- Give plenty of reassurance.
- Ride out with a calm pony.

ABOUT BOLTING

When a pony bolts, he's in a panic and is obeying his "flight" instinct, which is to run away. You need to work out what he's running away from, especially if he runs away with you often. He may be trying to escape pain in his teeth, so when you pull on the reins, you make it worse. If you are riding badly, he may be trying to escape you banging on his back. It's also possible that he's just spotted something very scary.

Half-halt

Give

If your pony bolts, don't panic. He is already frightened, so screaming or clinging on will make him worse.

Sit up straight and deep into the saddle. Remind him you're there by giving and taking with the reins.

Half-halt again

Try turning him in a big circle. This may gradually slow him down and get him to take notice of you again.

DEALING WITH NAPPING

Napping is when you can't make your pony go forwards or do what you want. He may try to turn back home or run backwards. He may be in pain, afraid, or confused from being given mixed messages. He may feel vulnerable at being asked to do things on his own. It's also possible that he's bored, or thinks he's boss.

Don't let a nappy pony think he can boss you around.

What to do
* Watch for early signs of napping, such as playing up, throwing his head around and not moving forward willingly.
* Give him basic retraining to build his confidence and obedience.
* Keep his work varied and ride him strongly.
* Do some work on your own riding skills.

TRYING TO BUCK YOU OFF

This pony has his head down, so it's difficult for the rider to control him.

Ponies buck occasionally to let off steam, but frequent bucking can be a problem. It's a pony's way of shaking off a predator, so if his back hurts, he may be trying to buck the pain away. If there are no sores under his saddle have him checked by an expert. If he's a very high-spirited pony, he may just have found that it's a quick way to get rid of his rider.

What to do
* Cut down on concentrate Give him plenty of exercise
* Get back on if he bucks you off, so he knows he can't get rid of you.
* Keep his head up and you legs on if he's about to buck

REASONS FOR REARING

A pony may rear because he's in pain, confused or startled by something. You need to find out what's wrong very quickly, as once it's a habit it's very difficult to cure. Don't try to deal with it yourself - always get expert help. A pony that rears is dangerous to ride, because there is the risk of him falling over backwards on top of you.

What to do
- If possible, have him retrained by an expert so that he learns not to rear.
- If he rears while you're riding him, don't balance by pulling on the reins. This may pull him over on top of you.
- Lean forward, then as he comes down again, drive him forward strongly with your legs.

HANDLING PROBLEMS

Problem	Cause	Solution
Hard to catch	*Not enough time turned out. Not enough time with pony friends. Doesn't trust you or want to be with you. Knows he can get the better of you.*	*Allow plenty of time turned out with pony friends. Work on your relationship with him. Reward him for being caught with plenty of praise, so he sees it as a pleasant experience. Show you're herd leader by ignoring him when he looks interested in you. Walk away - he may follow. Last resort - leave his headcollar on so it's easier to catch hold of him.*
Hard to load	*Hasn't been trained properly and still sees trailer as dark, unsafe spooky place. Has had bad experience in trailer in the past. He's playing up.*	*May need retraining - allow him plenty of time to sniff around the trailer and get used to looking into it. Try loading him along with a calm experienced pony - he may follow him in. Tempt him in with titbits and reward him for each step in the right direction.*
Hard to tack up	*Saddle - Pain in back. Associates being ridden with a bad experience. His backing training wasn't completed properly.* *Bridle - Pain in mouth. May be head-shy through being hit on the head or having head roughly handled.*	*Have his back and saddle checked. Take him back to a basic level of training until he is comfortable with the saddle and with weight on his back.* *Have his teeth checked. Retrain with gentle handling of head with hand, gradually increasing the amount of contact, until he accepts it without a fuss.*
Hard to mount	*He has pain in his back from weight of rider. Associates being ridden with bad experience. He's just playing up.*	*If he's afraid or in pain, problems are likely to continue during riding. If so, have his back and saddle checked. If he's just playing up, don't let him get away with it. Ask for help in making him stand still.*

PARTNERSHIP

Getting to know and understand your pony forms the basis for all good riding partnerships, even if you just want to ride for fun. You can also build on your partnership if you want to keep on learning, or enter competitions.

RIDING FOR FUN

Once your pony sees you as his friend and leader, he'll enjoy your company and be loyal, too. However, if you only ride for fun make sure you don't take him for granted. He still needs a routine and regular exercise You must also avoid sloppy riding, so that he doesn't develop bad or lazy habits.

Hacking tips

* Don't relax your riding skills because you're not in a school. He still needs clear messages about what you want him to do.
* Don't let him get away with napping. Ride him along different routes so that he can't take control of where he's going.
* Keep him confident. Let him inspect anything scary or new that you come across

Try to vary where you canter. If you always canter in the same place he may start setting off before you tell him to.

FURTHER SCHOOLING AND DRESSAGE

To develop your pony's schooling and your own riding skills, you should ride regularly and continue taking lessons. Gradually, you will learn to feel and understand your pony's body and movements, so that you can work on quite subtle changes.

Once you get on to more advanced work, remember that each pony's ability is different and that some progress faster than others. If he is finding something difficult to learn, you may be asking too much of him, or pushing him too fast.

Dressage involves moves such as this pirouette in walk.

Dressage is really another way of saying training, and the work you do on your paces and transitions around the school is basic dressage work. The aims of dressage are to

help the pony move naturally and gracefully and for the rider and pony to achieve the greatest harmony possible. The pony can then respond to the lightest of aids.

COMPETING

A happy, lively pony will want to please you and may well enjoy showing off, too. Entering competitions is a great way of letting him do both. As well as dressage, you could try gymkhanas, show jumping, cross-country or showing. Before you decide which to try, assess your pony's strengths and weaknesses - his size, shape and temperament, and how skilful he is. Think about your own skills, too.

Tips for competing

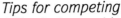

- Don't destroy his confidence by entering him for a competition that is too difficult for him.
- Don't ever punish him for losing, especially if he tried his best.
- Shows can be stressful places, so bear in mind that he may get nervous or over-excited. Keep him calm and give him plenty of reassurance.
- Make sure he is well prepared and fit enough, so that he doesn't strain himself on the day.

If he is small and keen, he may make a good gymkhana pony.

KEEPING ONE STEP AHEAD

However well you and your pony get on, remember that you can never predict exactly how he will behave. It's also important to realize that you can't know everything there is to know, and that you may sometimes need advice from people with more experience. Most important of all, remember that your pony depends on you for nearly all his needs, and he can't tell you when something's wrong. It's up to you to notice, and put it right.

If your pony is bold and enjoys jumping, you could enter him in cross-country competitions.

INDEX

With thanks to Victoria Barnes, Clare Davies, Ria Hollands,
Fionnula, Ginger, Lady and Solly

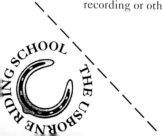